Date Due

FEB 5 1993	FEB 1 2 1994		**k**
FEB 1 7 1984			
MAY 1 4 1985	MAR 1 2 1994		
JUN 3 0 1987			
APR 2 4 1990			

About Starters

Starters books are written and designed with young readers in mind. They are vocabulary controlled and the contents have been carefully checked by a critic reader and teacher panel.

Each book contains questions for teacher-directed learning, bright and simple illustrations, interesting and informative text, picture glossary and a table of facts.

ISBN 0-88874-304-1

Edited by: GLC Editorial Department
Illustrations: Sigrid Schmitt
Critic Reader: Mrs. Margaret Knechtel, Reading Consultant,
Etobicoke Board of Education
Teacher Panel: Miss Grace Davis, Grade 2 Teacher,
John D. Parker Junior Public School,
Etobicoke Board of Education
Miss Maribel Hanson, Grade 2 Teacher,
Buttonwood Hill Junior Public School,
Etobicoke Board of Education

Printed by: Ashton-Potter Limited
Film preparation: Graphic Litho-plate Inc.
Bound by: The Hunter Rose Company Ltd.

Printed and Bound in Canada

Uniquely Canadian Materials from GLC Publishers Limited
115 Nugget Avenue
Agincourt, Ontario

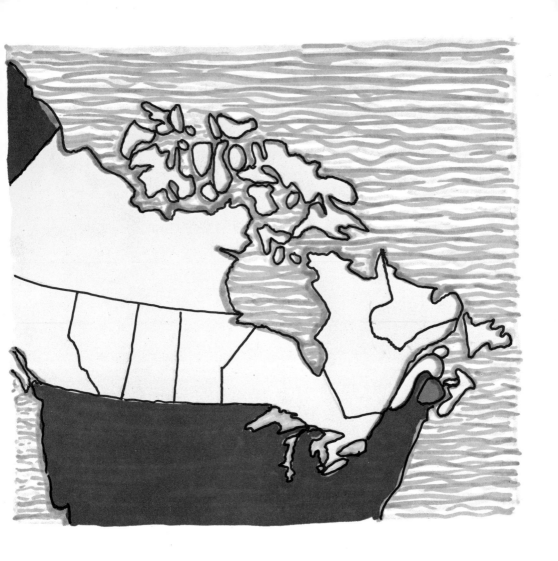

New Brunswick is one of the Maritime Provinces.
"Maritime" means "near the ocean".
The Maritimes are also called
the Atlantic Provinces.

Fredericton is the capital city
of New Brunswick.
It is on the banks of the St. John River.
Beautiful elm trees grow along
many of the city streets.

The Legislative Assembly Building
was built in 1880.
The government of New Brunswick works here.

Saint John is the biggest city in New Brunswick.
It is also the oldest city in Canada.
You can see many buildings
more than one hundred years old.

4

Cars seem to coast up Magnetic Hill in Moncton.
Moncton is the second largest city
in New Brunswick.
Many people who live in Moncton speak French.

A ferry takes visitors to Grand Manan Island.
It is a good place to watch whales,
gather seashells, or lie on the beach.

6

These big rocks look like huge flowerpots.
Some of them are fifteen metres high.

Many people come to New Brunswick
for their holidays.

8

What would you like to do
on a holiday in New Brunswick?

Many places in New Brunswick have festivals
in the summer.
Shediac has a Lobster Festival.
Campbellton has a Salmon Festival.

10

Folk dancing and singing are part of the
Miramichi Folk Song Festival in Newcastle.

These fishermen are catching
many different kinds of fish.
They catch cod, herring,
and Atlantic salmon.

12

Lobsters are trapped and put into
these lobster pounds.
Fresh lobsters are shipped to markets
all over the world.

These miners are digging for minerals.
They break off big pieces of rock.

These lumberjacks are cutting down trees.
The best trees go to sawmills
to be made into lumber.
Other trees go to a pulpmill
to be made into newsprint.

These things are made in factories
in New Brunswick.

Here is a large chocolate factory.

Potatoes

Potatoes are the most important crop
in New Brunswick.
In some places, schools open in August
and close in September so the children
can help with the potato harvest.

18

Fiddleheads are young ferns.

Fiddleheads are picked in the early spring.

When they are boiled, fiddleheads are good to eat.

Peat moss is gathered from the bogs
near Shippegan.
Peat moss is sometimes mixed with garden soil.
It makes the soil better for growing plants.

20

Dulse is a seaweed which is picked from rocks
when the tide is out.
It is dried in the sun.
People eat it raw or toast it over a fire.

There are several covered bridges
in New Brunswick.
This is the longest one in the world.
Cross this bridge holding your breath
and your wish comes true.

22

LONG AGO

Micmac Indians lived in New Brunswick.

In spring and summer they fished in the ocean.

In fall and winter they moved inland to hunt.

LONG AGO

The Acadians are French people.
They came to live in New Brunswick.
They built small farms by building dikes
to keep out the sea.

24

Picture Glossary

Legislative Assembly Building
(page 3)

lobster
(page 10)

festival
(page 10)

salmon
(page 10)

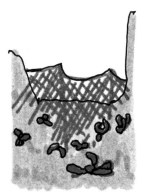

lobster pound
(page 13)

peat moss
(page 20)

fiddleheads
(page 19)

dulse
(page 21)